WHO'S THE GOAT?
USING MATH TO CROWN THE CHAMPION™

I0805307

RONALDO VS MESSI VS BECKHAM VS PELÉ

Carla Mooney

rosen publishing's
rosen central®
New York

Published in 2020 by The Rosen Publishing Group, Inc.
29 East 21st Street, New York, NY 10010

Copyright © 2020 by The Rosen Publishing Group, Inc.

First Edition

All rights reserved. No part of this book may be reproduced in any form without permission in writing from the publisher, except by a reviewer.

Library of Congress Cataloging-in-Publication Data

Names: Mooney, Carla, author.
Title: Ronaldo vs. Messi vs. Beckham vs. Pelé / Carla Mooney.
Other titles: Ronaldo versus Messi versus Beckham versus Pelé
Description: First edition. | New York : Rosen Publishing, 2020. | Series: Who's the GOAT? Using math to crown the champion | Audience: Grades: 5 to 8. | Includes bibliographical references and index.
Identifiers: LCCN 2019009431| ISBN 9781725348509 (library bound) | ISBN 9781725348493 (pbk.)
Subjects: LCSH: Ronaldo, Cristiano, 1985- —Juvenile literature. | Messi, Lionel, 1987- —Juvenile literature. | Beckham, David, 1975- —Juvenile literature. | Pelé, 1940- —Juvenile literature. | Soccer players—Biography—Juvenile literature. | Soccer players—Rating of—Juvenile literature. | Soccer players—Statistics—Juvenile literature.
Classification: LCC GV942.7.A1 M644 2020 | DDC 796.3340922 [B]—dc23
LC record available at https://lccn.loc.gov/2019009431

Manufactured in the United States of America

CONTENTS

INTRODUCTION

Globally, soccer is the king of all sports. According to some estimates, more than half of the people on the planet consider themselves to be soccer fans, an estimated four billion people. In the words of Bill Shankly, who managed England's Liverpool Football Club in the 1960s and 1970s, "Some people believe football [soccer] is a matter of life and death, I am very disappointed with that attitude. I can assure you it is much, much more important than that."

Though soccer's ancient beginnings can be traced all the way back to second-century China, the modern game originated in England—and spread throughout the world. The sport as it is known today matches two teams of eleven players, plus a goaltender, against each other on a large, grassy field. Each team tries to kick a ball into the goal net, which is defended by the opposing team. As they run across the field, players use their feet—and sometimes their heads—to move the ball. Aside from the goaltender, players are not permitted to use their hands to touch the ball.

With so many dedicated, passionate followers of the game, it is hard to find a single clear answer to any of soccer's big questions—the biggest of which is: who is the greatest player of all time, the GOAT? The answer divides soccer experts, fans, and generations.

The debate over who owns the title of soccer's GOAT is hotly debated in coffee shops and soccer stadiums, on radio and television shows, and in locker rooms around the world. Everyone has their own argument for why their favorite superstar is the GOAT. Some fans argue that Portugal's Cristiano Ronaldo is the greatest player in history. Others insist that Argentina's Lionel Messi owns the title. Has anyone ever been able to "bend it" like England's David Beckham? No conversation about soccer's greatest player could be complete without including Brazil's Pelé, the only player ever to win three World Cup championships for his country.

To figure out an answer to soccer's GOAT question, most fans and experts turn to facts and figures. The number of goals scored is an important statistic—but is it the only one that is important when evaluating a player's career? What about a player's longevity, how many games and minutes he played? What is his strike rate or goals per game? Perhaps most importantly—from a fan's point of view—how did the player perform when the stage was the biggest and the pressure was the highest? While the numbers might not reveal a single obvious winner, they may help fans reach their own conclusions about which soccer player has earned the title of the GOAT.

CHAPTER 1

PORTUGAL'S GREATEST: CRISTIANO RONALDO

On February 5, 1985, Maria Delores dos Santos and José Dinis Aveiro welcomed their fourth child, a son. They named him Cristiano Ronaldo dos Santos Aveiro. The family lived on the Portuguese island of Madeira. From an early age, soccer was a big part of Ronaldo's life. His father worked as an equipment manager for the local soccer club, Andorinha. Young Ronaldo often went with his father to work, always bringing a soccer ball along with him. He could commonly be found practicing dribbling like the professional players or playing soccer in the street with his friends.

A QUICK "LITTLE BEE"

With his father's encouragement, eight-year-old Ronaldo joined Andorinha's youth soccer team. Even at that young age, Ronaldo's talent was clear. Not only was he naturally faster and more athletic than his competition, he also had great ball handling skills. Ronaldo was small and very quick and was given the nickname "little bee."

It was not long before other Madeira-based soccer clubs noticed Ronaldo. Nacional, the island's biggest team, invited him to join the club in 1995, when he was only ten years old. Soon, Ronaldo's talent attracted the attention of clubs outside of Madeira. A scout for Sporting CP, a club based in Lisbon, Portugal, spotted him and offered Ronaldo a spot in the club's soccer academy. Sporting CP was one of the biggest soccer clubs in Portugal. In 1997, at age twelve, Ronaldo moved from Madeira to Lisbon.

Sporting CP took a chance on Cristiano Ronaldo, and Portugal—not to mention the entire soccer world—greatly benefited from it.

In 2002, Ronaldo was promoted to Sporting CP's senior team. In October of that year, he made his debut in the Primeira Liga, the top division in Portugal's soccer league. His play on the soccer field drew the attention of prominent soccer clubs in England, including Liverpool, Arsenal, and Manchester United. In 2003, Ronaldo and Sporting CP played in a UEFA (Union of European Football Associations) Champions League game against Manchester United. In the match, Ronaldo's footwork and skill impressed Sir Alex Ferguson, Manchester United's manager. Ferguson believed Ronaldo to be one of the most exciting young players he had ever watched. Manchester negotiated a deal with Sporting CP to sign Ronaldo for more than $14 million—a record amount for a player so young.

Cristiano Ronaldo (*right*) is shown here talking with Sir Alex Ferguson, the man who discovered him.

CR7, THE MOST EXPENSIVE PLAYER IN THE WORLD

Ronaldo started playing for Manchester United in the 2003–2004 season. Although he initially asked for the number 28 jersey, he was given number 7, which had been worn previously by Manchester United legend David Beckham. The new number, combined with his initials, quickly became his worldwide nickname: CR7.

In the Premier League with Manchester United, Ronaldo immediately became a star. During Ronaldo's time with the team, he led the club to several titles, including three Premier League titles, two Football League Cups, the 2004 FA (Football Association) Cup Championship, and the UEFA Champions League and FIFA (Fédération Internationale de Football Association) World Cup championships in 2008. He was also named the FIFA World Player of the Year in 2008. These accomplishments at such a young age were truly remarkable. In 2009, attracted by Ronaldo's quickly expanding résumé, Spanish powerhouse soccer club Real Madrid paid Manchester United $105 million to bring him to Spain. This deal made him the most expensive player in the world. Although the pressure to perform was high, Ronaldo excelled with Real Madrid. Between 2009 and 2018, Ronaldo became Real Madrid's top goal scorer of all time.

A CHAMPION'S LEAGUE

The UEFA Champions League is an annual soccer tournament organized by the Union of European Football Associations. The top clubs of the numerous European soccer leagues compete in this prestigious tournament every year, each vying for the cup. Europe's strongest leagues are permitted to enter up to five teams into the tournament. The tournament begins with thirty-two teams divided into eight groups. In this group stage, teams play others in the same group in a round-robin format from September to December. The group winners and runners-up move on to a knockout round beginning in February. The final occurs in late May. Real Madrid—assisted in the twenty-first century by Cristiano Ronaldo—has won the title a record thirteen times and was the 2018 champion.

Every year, the UEFA Champions League competition brings together the top European soccer clubs to compete for the title of Europe's best club.

In 2012, Ronaldo led the team to his first Spanish league title. He followed that up with three UEFA Champions League titles in 2014, 2016, and 2017 and another La Liga title in 2017. During this time, Ronaldo demonstrated again and again to the world that he was a prolific and proficient goal scorer, with more than 100 total goals over the next three years.

PLAYING FOR PORTUGAL

At the 2006 World Cup tournament, Ronaldo was an important part of Portugal's national team. He scored one goal during the tournament and the team advanced to the semifinals. In 2007, Ronaldo was named the Portuguese national team's captain. He led the team in several World Cup tournaments (2006, 2010, 2014, and 2018) and European Championships (2004, 2008, 2012, and 2016). In 2016, Ronaldo and the Portugal team captured the European Championship.

In 2018, Ronaldo shocked the soccer world and announced that he would be leaving Real Madrid to join the Italian soccer club Juventus. He now has the opportunity to win a European league title with a third team, which would be another incredible achievement to add to his long list of successes.

IS RONALDO THE GREATEST?

In addition to team trophies, Ronaldo has earned an impressive number of individual awards. He is a five-time winner of the FIFA Ballon d'Or trophy, an award given each year to the world's best male soccer player.

Only Ronaldo and Argentina's Lionel Messi have won this award five times, tying each other for the record.

Ronaldo has also been selected as the UEFA Best Player in Europe four times. He has won scoring titles sixteen times and was chosen as the Player of the Year in the Champions League in 2008.

In 2015, the Portuguese Football Federation named Ronaldo the greatest Portuguese player of all time, ranking him ahead of other greats Eusébio and Luís Figo. A look at his stats further illustrates his impressive career. First of all, Ronaldo is known as one of the world's best goal scorers. From his professional debut in 2002 through February 19, 2019, he has scored a career total of 677 goals. He has played in 944 games—790 for his club teams and 154 for the Portugal national team. This means that he has a strike rate of .71 goals per game. Strike rate is an important statistic that represents how often a player is able to score goals. This rate can be calculated by dividing a player's number of goals by the number of games in which he or she has played. For Ronaldo:

$$677 \div 944 = .71$$

A career strike rate of .71 is impressive, but looking a little closer at these numbers shows how dominant Ronaldo truly is. He is the only player in history to score fifty or more goals in six different club seasons. In most of these seasons, he averaged more than a goal per game:

Season	Goals scored		Games played		Strike rate
2010–2011	53	÷	54	=	.98
2011–2012	60	÷	55	=	1.09
2012–2013	55	÷	55	=	1.00
2013–2014	51	÷	47	=	1.09
2014–2015	61	÷	54	=	1.13
2015–2016	51	÷	48	=	1.06

Not only is Ronaldo great at scoring goals, he is also good at setting up his teammates to score. In his career, Ronaldo has had 212 assists for club teams in 790 games. A player earns an assist when she or he passes the ball to a teammate who scores a goal. For Portugal's national team, Ronaldo has 37 assists in 154 games. To figure out his average assists per game, add his total number of assists and divide that sum by the sum of his career club games and his career national games:

- 212 + 37 = 249
- 790 + 154 = 944
- 249 ÷ 944 = .26

Based on these calculations, Ronaldo averages .26 assists per game.

Some other numbers can help reveal how accurate Ronaldo's shot is. In his complete 2017–2018 season,

Cristiano Ronaldo is shown here celebrating after scoring one of his many goals for Real Madrid.

he took 251 shots. Of those, 108 were on goal and had to be stopped by the goaltender. Using these stats, it is possible to figure out that his shooting accuracy was 43 percent. This is calculated by taking the number of shots on goal and dividing that by the total shots:

108 ÷ 251 = .43 (43 percent)

Because this calculation is used to find a percentage, move the decimal point two places to the right. Ronaldo's strong 43 percent accuracy rate means that nearly every other shot he takes is accurate enough to reach the goal.

Additionally, of the 251 shots Ronaldo took in 2017–2018, 42 of them resulted in goals. Therefore, he scored on 16.7 percent of his shots. This is calculated by dividing his goals by the total number of shots he took:

42 ÷ 251 = .167 (16.7 percent)

This percentage reflects his overall shot success rate, but even more impressive is his scoring rate in shots on goal of 38.9 percent (42 ÷ 108 = .389).

With stats like these, Portugal's Cristiano Ronaldo is seen by many as one of the world's best active soccer players. His dominating performances on the pitch for more than a decade—along with numerous team and countless individual awards—have solidified his legacy as one of the best, if not the greatest, in the game.

CHAPTER 2

TOP SCORER: LIONEL MESSI

On June 24, 1987, Lionel Andrés Messi, the third son of Celia Cuccittini and Jorge Messi, was born. The working-class family lived in Rosario, Argentina. On his fourth birthday, Lionel's parents gave him a white soccer ball with red diamonds. With the new ball, he decided to join his father and older brothers playing soccer in the street. Even then, his talent was unmistakable—and it has gotten only more impressive with age.

A LITTLE BOY WITH A BIG TALENT

Young Messi joined the youth team for the local soccer club, Newell's Old Boys, at age six. Both of his older brothers had played youth soccer for the team as well. In his first game with Newell's, Messi scored four goals in a 6–0 win. Even as a young athlete, his explosiveness set him apart from his teammates.

As a child, however, Messi was noticeably smaller than other boys his age. At age nine, doctors diagnosed him with a growth hormone deficiency. The good news, however, was that the condition could be treated. Doctors prescribed daily injections of human growth hormone—an expensive treatment that cost several hundred dollars per month.

Meanwhile, Messi's impressive youth play had caught the attention of European clubs. FC Barcelona gave him a trial and he impressed the coaches. FC Barcelona offered him a contract and agreed to pay for his medical bills if he moved to Spain and enrolled in Barcelona's youth soccer academy. When Messi was thirteen years old, he and his father moved to Spain, and his career began.

A young and talented Lionel Messi played with the under-twenty Argentine soccer team in the FIFA World Youth Championships.

BREAKING OUT IN BARCELONA

In Barcelona, Messi quickly moved up through the club's junior teams. In October 2004, he made his debut in La Liga, Spain's premier soccer league. In the 2004–2005 season, he played seventy-seven minutes (out of a possible ninety) for the first team and scored his first goal in May 2005 against Albacete. At age seventeen, he was the youngest player ever to score in a La Liga game for Barcelona.

In 2006, Messi and Barcelona won both the La Liga and the UEFA Champions League. In his first Champions League tournament, Messi scored six goals in seventeen appearances. However, a muscle tear in his thigh sidelined him while Barcelona went on to win the championship game.

In the 2006–2007 season, Messi earned a spot on Barcelona's top eleven-member team. Over the season, he became an essential fixture and top striker for Barcelona. In each successive season with the team, Messi continued to improve, becoming a breakout star. In 2009, Messi won his first Copa del Rey with Barcelona, an annual knockout soccer competition organized by the Royal Spanish Football Federation. He also led Barcelona to win the La Liga and the UEFA Champions League in 2009. With three championships in a single year, Barcelona became Spain's first club to win the treble. A treble, in the soccer world, is any season in which a single team wins three championship titles. That same year, Messi won his first FIFA Ballon d'Or, the award given to the best player of the year.

In 2011–2012, Messi shattered several records with his incredible play. For the second time, he was the top goal scorer in La Liga, with a record-setting fifty goals. In addition, he became the first player to score five goals in a single UEFA Champions League match. For the fourth consecutive time, Messi earned his spot as the Champions League top scorer, scoring fourteen goals in the tournament. Over the entire 2011–2012 season, Messi scored seventy-three goals and had twenty-nine assists across all club matches—more than any other player in the history of soccer. Even more impressive, Messi broke the all-time world record for the most goals scored for club and country in a calendar year. His ninety-one total goals eclipsed the previous record of eighty-five by German Gerd Müller and Pelé's iconic seventy-five goals in 1958. Messi's outstanding play led Barcelona to renew its contract with the star until 2018.

In 2014, he became the all-time leading scorer in La Liga and Champions League play. In 2015, he helped Barcelona win its second treble. Also in 2015, Messi was honored for his incredible play with a record fifth Ballon d'Or trophy. The

Lionel Messi is shown here with four of his record-tying five FIFA Ballon d'Or trophies. Is that enough to make him the GOAT?

A LUCRATIVE CAREER

The position of soccer superstar has always been well paid. There are three soccer players ranked in the top five on the *Forbes* 2018 list of the world's highest-paid athletes. Lionel Messi comes in second, earning salary and winnings of $84 million and endorsements of $27 million in 2018, for a total of $111 million (84 million + 27 million = 111 million). Cristiano Ronaldo is right behind Messi on the list at third. Ronaldo earned $61 million in salary and winnings and $47 million in endorsements in 2018, a total of $108 million (61 million + 47 million = 108 million). The third soccer player, Neymar from Brazil, comes in at fifth; he earned $73 million in salary and winnings and $17 million in endorsements during the year, for a total of $90 million (73 million + 17 million = 90 million).

only other player to win five of these prestigious awards is Cristiano Ronaldo.

With Barcelona, Messi has won numerous championships through 2018, including four UEFA Champions League titles and nine La Liga championships. He has also won eight Spanish Super Cup titles, six Spanish Cup titles, and three FIFA Club World Cup titles. He truly is the champion's champion.

PLAYING FOR THE HOME COUNTRY

While playing for Barcelona, Messi has also been an integral player for Argentina's national team over the years. In 2005, he led Argentina to victory in the 2005 FIFA Youth Championship. In 2008, Messi won an Olympic gold medal for Argentina as a participant in the Beijing Summer Olympics.

A World Cup title is the one honor that has eluded Messi. In 2006, he played in his first World Cup and became Argentina's youngest player to play in the tournament. In 2014, Messi led Argentina to the World Cup finals. Although Argentina lost in the finals, Messi was named the player of the tournament, another impressive individual achievement.

In 2016, after Argentina lost to Chile in the finals of the Copa América tournament, Messi announced his retirement from his national team. The retirement was short-lived, however, as he returned for the 2018 World Cup tournament and one last shot at the championship. Unfortunately for Messi, Argentina was eliminated in the round of sixteen in a 4–3 loss to France, the eventual World Cup championship team. Messi produced two assists in the game, the first Argentinian player to do so in a World Cup game since Diego Maradona in 1986.

AN IMPRESSIVE CAREER, BY THE NUMBERS

Over his career, Messi has won numerous team trophies, established scoring records, and won an unbelievable number of individual awards. He shares the record for FIFA Ballon d'Or trophies—at five each—with Ronaldo.

Messi has been chosen as the UEFA Best Player in Europe three times. He has won scoring titles sixteen times and was chosen as the Player of the Year three times. Many fans of the game regard Messi as one of the most exciting, dynamic players ever.

A look at Messi through his career statistics shows that he has put together an impressive résumé. Like his rival Ronaldo, Messi is one of the world's best goal scorers. From his professional debut in 2004 through February 19, 2019, he has scored a career total of 647 goals in 796 games. This gives him a strike rate of .81 goals per game (647 ÷ 796 = .81).

Lionel Messi won an Olympic gold medal after Argentina defeated Nigeria at the 2008 Olympic Games in Beijing, China.

In his career, Messi has scored fifty or more goals in five different club seasons—one fewer than Ronaldo. In most of these seasons, he averaged more than a goal per game, close to Ronaldo's numbers.

Season	Goals scored		Games played		Strike rate
2010–2011	53	÷	55	=	.96
2011–2012	73	÷	60	=	1.22
2012–2013	60	÷	50	=	1.20
2014–2015	58	÷	57	=	1.02
2016–2017	54	÷	52	=	1.04

Over his career, Messi has struggled with injuries. From his debut in 2004 to February 2019, he has missed ninety-four games. How many goals did he miss out on during these games? To calculate this hypothetical number, multiply Messi's career strike rate by the number of games in which he has not played:

$$.81 \times 94 = 76.1$$

Based on this calculation, it is reasonable to assume that if Messi had been healthy for his entire career, he would have scored an additional seventy-six goals. Adding this hypothetical goal total to his career scoring, it can be estimated that his career goals could have been 723 if not for injuries (647 + 76 = 723).

When not scoring goals, Messi is also adept at assisting his teammates in scoring. In his career, Messi

Despite his undeniable skill and impressive statistics, Messi has been plagued by injuries throughout his career.

has 276 assists for club and national teams in 796 games. This gives him an impressive average of .35 assists per game (276 ÷ 796 = .35).

How accurate is Messi at shooting the ball? In the 2017–2018 season, he took 239 shots. Of those, 119 were on goal. His shooting accuracy was, therefore, 49.8 percent (119 ÷ 239 = .498). Of the 239 shots taken, Messi scored 44 times, or 18.4 percent of the shots he took (44 ÷ 239 = .184), and 37 percent of his shots on goal (44 ÷ 119 = .37). Both of these stats are right on pace with Ronaldo's performances.

In the minds of many soccer and sports fans, Argentina's Lionel Messi has been the best player in the world since he broke into the pros. His record-setting performances for Barcelona and Argentina continue to amaze fans, coaches, and fellow soccer players.

CHAPTER 3

ENGLAND'S ICON: DAVID BECKHAM

On May 2, 1975, David Robert Joseph Beckham was born to Ted and Sandra Beckham in Leytonstone, London, England. The middle child between two sisters, David grew up in a middle-class family. Together, the Beckham family rooted for Manchester United, England's legendary soccer club.

Like most soccer greats, Beckham's skill and potential emerged from an early age. He spent many hours kicking a soccer ball with his father at a local park. Around age eight, he joined a local youth team called the Ridgeway Rovers. By age ten, he had scored 100 goals. When he was only eleven years old, he won the prestigious Bobby Charlton Soccer Schools National Skills competition. His talent soon caught the eye of bigger clubs around England. In 1990, while playing for the Brimsdown Rovers youth team, David was named the Under-15 Player of the Year.

MANCHESTER UNITED'S YOUNG STAR

David's skill soon caught the eye of Manchester United officials. In 1991, he signed a youth training contract. At age sixteen, David left home to play for Manchester United's youth training division. At Manchester, he excelled in the youth academy. In 1992, he helped the club win the FA Youth Cup. His stellar performance in the cup matches led to him getting a call-up in 1992 to play with Manchester United's first team as a substitute. Shortly after, Beckham signed a professional contract with Manchester in January 1993.

After several call-ups to the first team in the 1993–1994 seasons, Manchester sent Beckham on loan to another team—Preston North End—for part of the 1994–1995 season. Preston, unlike Manchester, was in the second tier of England's soccer league. Playing for their first team would give Beckham more experience, though not against top-rate competition. At first, Beckham was skeptical. He was worried this "demotion" to

As a child, David Beckham grew up rooting for the Manchester United soccer club—and would eventually play for them.

Preston meant the team no longer wanted to deal with him. However, his time with Preston helped to shape his early career. With the lower-tier club, he played more minutes and was given more responsibility on the field. Beckham embraced the challenge, scoring two goals in five appearances.

When he returned to Manchester in 1995, Beckham joined the first team. He played as the right side attacking midfielder. Before long, Beckham became an integral part of Manchester United. Under his leadership, the team was a force in English soccer. In 1999, Beckham and Manchester United won the treble, winning three championships—the Premier League, the FA Cup, and the UEFA Champions League—in the same year. Also in 1999, Beckham was named the UEFA Best Player in Europe.

During his time with Manchester United, Beckham became one of the world's greatest midfielders. In eight years, he scored goals in 262 games and won six Premier League titles, the FA Cup twice, and the UEFA Champions League in 1999.

ENGLAND'S NATIONAL TEAM

In 1996, Beckham debuted for England's national team. He quickly became a first-team regular. In 1998, Beckham played for England in the World Cup. In his first World

Beckham, as England's midfielder, is shown here looking to pass the ball during the 1998 World Cup Finals.

Cup, Beckham scored a phenomenal free kick against Colombia in the group stages. In the round of sixteen, England faced Argentina. After being fouled, Beckham retaliated by kicking his leg out, and he was ejected from the tournament. Although England tied Argentina at the end of regular time, they ended up losing the match in penalty shots. Many criticized Beckham's behavior.

In the next few years, however, Beckham would redeem himself in the eyes of English fans. In 2000, he became the captain of England's national team. In October 2001, he scored a last-minute goal in a World Cup qualifying match that allowed England to qualify for the 2002 World Cup. This time, England made it to the quarterfinals before being eliminated by Brazil, the tournament's eventual champion.

In 2006, Beckham played in his last World Cup tournament for England. He scored a free kick in the round-of-sixteen match against Ecuador. England moved on to the quarterfinals but was eliminated by Portugal in penalties. Over his career, Beckham played in 115 games for England and scored seventeen goals.

LEAVING ENGLAND

In 2003, Beckham left Manchester United for Real Madrid. There, he joined soccer stars Ronaldo, Luís Figo, Zinedine Zidane, and Roberto Carlos. Expectations after his signing were high. Beckham quickly won over fans with his precise passing and ability to strike the ball with power and accuracy. Within a few weeks of his arrival, the team won the Spanish Super Cup.

Over the next four years, Beckham played in 159 official matches and scored 10 goals for Real Madrid. In 2007, thirty-two-year-old Beckham capped his career with Real Madrid by winning the La Liga championship. This was yet another major milestone in a long, successful career.

In 2007, Beckham moved across the Atlantic Ocean to play for the Los Angeles Galaxy in America's Major League Soccer (MLS). He played for the team for five seasons. Part of the time, he was loaned out and played for Italy's AC Milan. Other times, he was limited because of injuries.

Beckham's best season with the Galaxy occurred in 2011. He set a new career high of fifteen assists in twenty-six regular season MLS matches and more than twenty assists across all competition. He showed no signs of slowing down, even in his twentieth season as a soccer professional, and remained one of the world's best players. He was named to the MLS All-Star Team for a second time. He was also named to the MLS Best XI (an annual list of the best eleven MLS players) and named the MLS Comeback Player of the Year. Beckham continued his strong play into the postseason. He scored an assist in all of LA's four playoff games and helped the team win the MLS Cup.

Beckham is shown here in one of his last games for the Los Angeles Galaxy, a playoff match against the Seattle Sounders.

In 2012, Beckham led the Galaxy back to the MLS Cup final. They defeated the Houston Dynamo, 3–1, to win a second championship. Prior to the final, Beckham announced that it would be his final game with the Galaxy—and with the victory, he went out with a bang.

A LAST STOP IN PARIS

In early 2013, Beckham signed a five-month contract with Paris Saint-Germain (PSG) in France Ligue 1. The international star also announced that his entire salary would be donated to a local children's charity. Beckham debuted for PSG in February 2013. In May 2013, Beckham helped the team win the French Ligue 1 title, beating Lyon 1–0. With this title, Beckham has won championships across four different leagues and with four different teams.

On May 16, 2013, Beckham announced that he was retiring from professional soccer at the end of the season. In his final game, a 3–1 victory, fans gave him a standing ovation. "I just feel that it's the right time. I feel that I've achieved everything that I could in my career. I wanted to go out as a champion," Beckham said in an article for *The Telegraph*.

FROM PLAYER TO OWNER

David Beckham announced the creation of his new Major League Soccer franchise in Miami, Florida, in 2018.

In 2018, David Beckham and his business partners were awarded a new MLS franchise in Miami, Florida. The team will be named Club Internacional de Fútbol Miami, or Inter Miami CF. The owners plan to build a 25,000-seat stadium in the Miami area to host the team. Beckham is the first former MLS player to go on to own a team. His experience and reputation in the soccer world are expected to help the new expansion team thrive in South Florida. The team is expected to be ready to play in 2020, though—in many sports—expansion teams require a few years to become competitive and contend for a league title. Under Beckham's leadership, however, anything is possible.

WHAT MAKES BECKHAM A GOAT?

For many fans, David Beckham is the one of the greatest soccer stars to play the game. He was a born leader and key member in every locker room for all of his teams. The importance of playing this role is often overlooked; sports teams often require a vocal player to excite, encourage, and teach other members of the team. On the field, Beckham's skills backed up his leadership position. Over his career, Beckham played in 830 games and scored 144 goals. This places his strike rate at .17 (144 ÷ 830 = .17). While this strike rate is not as impressive as Ronaldo's or Messi's, all of Beckham's contributions on the field cannot be measured by goals and assists. While Ronaldo, Messi, and Pelé played forward, Beckham primarily played as a midfielder. His role on the team was to move the ball from the defensive zone quickly and bring it up the field to the forwards, who would then drive toward the goal. As a result, it is expected that he would have fewer goals and assists. Instead, Beckham's strength was his ability to make teammates around him better. He is one of the game's greatest passers, able to get the ball to a teammate with remarkable accuracy.

CHAPTER 4

PELÉ'S BEAUTIFUL GAME

With three World Cup championships for Brazil, Pelé is considered by many people to be the greatest soccer player in history. Even among nonfans, his name is well known. Throughout his career, Pelé averaged almost a goal per game. He could strike the ball with either foot and was adept at anticipating what opponents were going to do on the field. He could also drop deep, pass cleanly, and dribble past opposing players. Paolo Amaral, the fitness trainer for Brazil's national team in 1958, described Pelé's incredible skills: "He could shoot with his left, with his right, and he had such vision that as soon as he got the ball, he already knew what he was going to do with it. He was extraordinary."

EARLY YEARS

On October 23, 1940, Edson Arantes do Nascimento (known as Pelé) was born in Três Corações, Minas Gerais, Brazil. His parents chose his name after American inventor Thomas Edison. Pelé grew up in São Paulo, Brazil, where his father taught him how to play soccer. Because the family was poor, Pelé could not afford to buy a soccer ball. Instead, he practiced with a sock stuffed full of newspapers.

As a child, Pelé played in indoor soccer leagues. Playing on smaller indoor fields helped develop his reaction speed. He quickly rose through the youth leagues. At age fifteen, he was signed by Santos FC, a professional Brazilian soccer club.

At Santos, Pelé was a rising star on the field. While he was still fifteen, he scored his first professional goal. In his first season, Pelé scored thirty-six goals in twenty-nine matches. In his second season, he was even better, scoring fifty-eight goals in thirty-eight matches. That gave him an incredible strike rate of 1.53 (58 ÷ 38 = 1.53). By age sixteen, Pelé was the top scorer in the Brazilian league. He played for Santos for eighteen seasons, until the 1972–1973 season. During that time, he became the leading goal scorer in club history. He also led the team

Legendary Brazilian soccer player Pelé is shown here controlling the ball downfield during a match in 1958.

Jânio da Silva Quadros was such a soccer fan that he declared Pelé one of the country's national treasures.

to six Brazilian championships, two Copa Libertadores titles (in 1962 and 1963), and two Intercontinental Cups (in 1963 and 1964).

Pelé's incredible talent attracted European soccer clubs, and several asked him to join their teams. In 1961, Brazilian president Jânio da Silva Quadros made that impossible. He declared Pelé a national treasure, which prevented him from playing soccer for another country. Though some viewed this as a manipulative approach to keeping a sports star in place, Pelé was well compensated for staying and playing in Brazil.

WORLD CUP SUPERSTAR

As incredible as he was playing for Santos, some of Pelé's greatest moments occurred when he played for Brazil's national team. At age seventeen, a young and relatively unknown Pelé burst onto the national soccer stage during the 1958 World Cup tournament. A knee injury kept

PELÉ'S PROMISE

In 1950, ten-year-old Pelé was convinced—along with many other Brazilians—that Brazil's national team was talented enough to win the World Cup. He listened to the game on the radio with his father and his father's friends because they did not have a television. When the team lost in the tournament, many fans across Brazil were devastated. For the first time in his life, Pelé saw his father cry. Pelé did not understand why his father was crying. He told his father not to be sad and reassured him: he promised to one day win the World Cup for his father. Eight years later, Pelé would make good on his promise, winning the 1958 World Cup with Brazil.

him out of the first two games, but he returned for the final game of the group stage. He scored the only goal in the quarterfinal game against Wales, scored three goals in the semifinal against France, and added two more goals in the finals against Sweden. Aged seventeen, he became the youngest player to win a World Cup. He was also named the Young Player of the Tournament. Still a teenager, he was already exhibiting elite footwork, immense athleticism, and a true knack for scoring goals. These characteristics would define his entire career.

In 1962, Pelé helped Brazil repeat as World Cup champions. He was injured early on in the tournament and had to sit on the sidelines while his teammates successfully captured their title again. In 1966,

Pelé was happy after Brazil's 1958 World Cup Final against Sweden; in the match, he scored two of Brazil's five goals.

Pelé's Brazilian squad entered the tournament as favorites but lost in the group stage of the tournament. Bitterly disappointed by the defeat, Pelé decided to end his international career.

His retirement would not last, however, and Pelé returned to lead Brazil one more time in the 1970 World Cup. In the tournament, Pelé and the Brazilian team played incredibly well. Brazil scored nineteen goals in the tournament, the second-highest total ever by a World Cup winner. Pelé scored four goals and had six assists in the tournament, including a goal and two assists in Brazil's 4–1 defeat of Italy in the finals. With this win, Pelé became the only player in history to win three World Cups.

NEW YORK AND BEYOND

In 1974, Pelé announced his retirement from soccer. A year later, however, he agreed to play for the New York Cosmos in the North American Soccer League in the United States. Pelé's superstar status made the league a big attraction at the time. He played for three seasons and led the Cosmos to the US title in his final year, 1977. In his last game, Pelé played an exhibition between New York and Santos in 1977. He played one half for each team. Upon his retirement, he had scored an unbelievable 1,281 goals in 1,363 games.

Pelé was given a special Ballon d'Or award in 2013. He was not eligible for the award when he played, as it was given only to Europeans.

After his retirement, Pelé was named the FIFA Player of the Century and the Athlete of the Century by the International Olympic Committee. In 2013, FIFA honored the legendary player with a special Ballon d'Or in recognition of his remarkable career.

"THE KING OF FOOTBALL"

Throughout his career, Pelé amazed soccer fans throughout the world. He scored more than 1,000 goals over his career, a total that no modern player is even close to achieving. His career strike rate was an amazing .94 (1,281 ÷ 1,363 = .94). Many times, Pelé scored multiple times per game—something highly uncommon in soccer. Six times, he scored five goals in a single game. Thirty times, he scored four goals in a game, and he scored three goals in ninety-two matches. These numbers are all remarkable.

Pelé played decades before modern stars like Ronaldo and Messi. Today, soccer stars play approximately fifty to sixty club games each season. When Pelé played for Santos and the New York Cosmos, he played 542 games over 21 seasons, or only about 25 games per season. The games he played per season is calculated by dividing the number of games played by the number of seasons:

$$542 \div 21 = 25.8$$

He scored 535 goals during those games for a strike rate of .99 ($535 \div 542 = .99$). How good could Pelé have been if he had played in a season roughly twice as long? To start figuring out these hypothetical stats, multiply his number of seasons played by fifty (the number of games in a modern season): this produces 1,050 games ($21 \times 50 = 1{,}050$). This number can then be multiplied by his strike rate over those seasons to calculate a hypothetical number of goals:

$$1{,}050 \times .99 = 1{,}039.5$$

Therefore, if Pelé played in modern seasons, he would have scored an estimated 1,039.5 goals. This total is incredible. However, some may argue that it would be impossible for him to produce a strike rate of .99 across a much longer season. If his hypothetical goals are calculated using Pelé's career strike rate, he would still have scored an impressive 987 club goals (1,050 × .94 = 987).

For more than two decades, Pelé defined Brazilian soccer. Long before the internet and social media, Pelé became a global icon and nicknamed "Rei do Futebol," or the "King of Football." As Franz Beckenbauer—West Germany's 1974 FIFA World Cup–winning captain, who played alongside Pelé for New York Cosmos—said in an article on FIFA.com, "Pelé is the greatest player of all time. He reigned supreme for 20 years. All the others … rank beneath him. There's no one to compare with Pelé."

Pelé's love for the game took him all over the world; he is shown here shooting the ball for the New York Cosmos in 1977.

CHAPTER 5

WHAT DO THE NUMBERS SAY?

The eternal debate continues: who is the greatest soccer player of all time? Each of these four players—Ronaldo, Messi, Beckham, and Pelé—has a strong case as to why he should be crowned the best ever. Choosing among legendary players who played for different teams, during different times, is a nearly impossible task, but using statistics, both raw and calculated, can make the choice a little easier.

LOOKING AT THE NUMBERS

Soccer is mainly a game of goals and assists. Therefore, some of the most impactful players were the ones who were best able to find the back of the net. First, compare the total number of goals scored by each player:

- Ronaldo: 677 goals
- Messi: 647 goals
- Beckham: 144 goals
- Pelé: 1,281 goals

Pelé has the most goals by far. However, Ronaldo and Messi are actively playing well into the 2010s, so their goal totals will continue to increase. Because each player played in a different number of games, it is difficult to compare raw numbers of total goals. Instead, a better comparison might be the player's strike rate, or average goals per game.

- Ronaldo: .71 (677 ÷ 944 = .71)
- Messi: .81 (647 ÷ 796 = .81)
- Beckham: .17 (144 ÷ 830 = .17)
- Pelé: .94 (1,281 ÷ 1,363 = .94)

Here again, Pelé's strike rate is the best, as he averaged nearly a goal per game. Among the other players: although Ronaldo has more total goals than Messi, Messi's strike rate is higher; and Beckham's goals and strike rates are not a useful comparison because he was not a dedicated striker.

ROLE ON THE TEAM

As is obvious by looking at Beckham's total career stats, goals and assists do not tell the entire story about a player's impact on the field. Beckham's lower production can be explained by his different role on his team. Ronaldo, Messi, and Pelé are all forwards on the soccer field. In soccer, the team's forwards play nearest to the other team's goal. They are responsible for

Beckham's offensive statistics are not as flashy as some other players'—his true talents were in passing the ball and directing his team.

scoring goals and have limited defensive responsibilities. Because of their position and responsibilities on the field, forwards typically score more goals on the team than other players.

Unlike the other three players, Beckham played most of his career as a midfielder. His primary responsibility was ball handling and moving the ball up the field and passing it to the forwards on his team. As a result, it is to be expected that his goal statistics would be lower than the other players. Nonetheless, he brought an incredible amount of value to every team he played on—even if that value was not reflected in goals scored.

CLUB LEAGUE SUCCESS

Another measure of a player's greatness is his ability to lead his team to victory. Compare how often each player was able to lead his club team to a league championship:

- In eighteen seasons, Pelé's Santos team won six Brazilian championships. The team won an average of .33 championships per season. This is calculated by number of championships divided by number of seasons.

  $6 \div 18 = .33$

- Beckham won six Premier League championships, one La Liga title, three MLS titles, and one Ligue 1 title. Over twenty seasons and four leagues, he has eleven championships. This gives him an average of .55 titles per season ($11 \div 20 = .55$).
- Over fourteen completed seasons, Messi has won nine La Liga championships with Barcelona. This is an average of .64 championships per season ($9 \div 14 = .64$).
- Ronaldo has won the Premier League title three times with Manchester United in six

YELLOW VS. RED CARDS

In soccer, officials use colored cards to warn players against bad conduct. An official uses a yellow card to signal a warning to a player. If a player accumulates two yellow cards in a single match, he or she is ejected. The practice of using yellow and red cards in the World Cup did not surface until 1970, so Pelé does not have much of a penalty history.

Sometimes, officials use a red card to signal that a player has broken the rules and is being ejected from the game without warning. The ejected player must immediately leave the pitch and go to the dressing room. Their team is not permitted to substitute another player and must play the remainder of the game shorthanded.

Across his club career, Ronaldo has received 95 yellow cards, 4 second yellow cards, and 7 red cards. In comparison, Messi has received 68 yellow cards and no second yellow or red cards in club play. He received one red card early in his career while playing on the national team

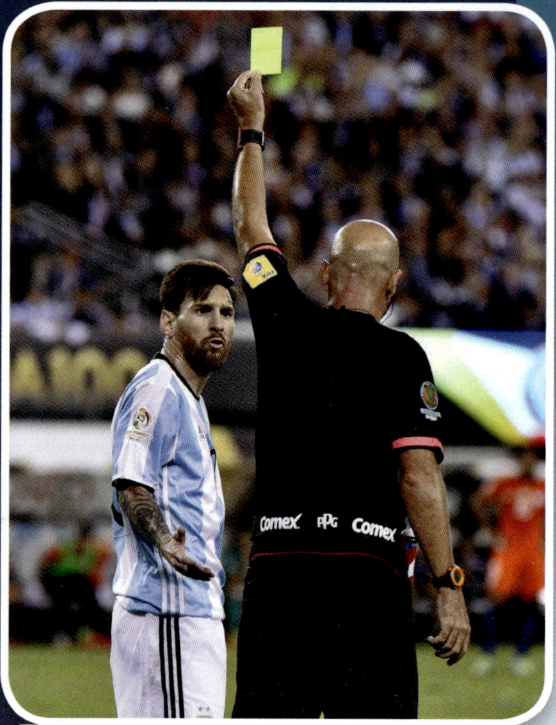

Argentina's Lionel Messi was given a yellow card warning during the Copa América Centenario final in 2016.

and has not repeated the mistake since. Beckham accumulated 109 yellow cards and 7 red cards during his career; these higher totals are not because he is a particularly dirty player, but because of the position he played on the pitch.

seasons and the La Liga title two times with Real Madrid in nine seasons. This gives him 5 championships in 15 seasons and an average of .33 titles per season (5 ÷ 15 = .33).

Using this measure, Beckham has won the most league championships, with eleven total titles. Although Messi's total of 9 is fewer than Beckham's, his average is higher at .64 per season. It is useful to compare the players on the basis of championships or title victories because soccer, after all, is a team sport. Looking at a team-based stat can help provide a greater understanding of the importance each of these players has had to his teams.

INTERNATIONAL SUCCESS

The pinnacle of success in soccer is winning the World Cup. Unlike many other sports' world championships, the prestigious World Cup tournament is held only every four years. Because there are fewer opportunities to win, victory is that much sweeter for the champions. For fans, the World Cup is the biggest sporting event on the planet. Where the Super Bowl—North America's biggest sporting event—draws hundreds of millions of viewers, the World Cup final match draws in billions. Passionate fans from dozens of countries all over the globe are glued to their television sets to see the two best international teams duke it out. Amid the frenzy of waving flags and national chants, legends are born at the World Cup.

Pelé is the only player in the history of soccer to have won three World Cup championships. He played in four tournaments and won three. This gives him an amazing win percentage of .750. Winning percentage is calculated by dividing a player's number of wins by the number of games or tournaments:

$3 \div 4 = .750$

Ronaldo, Messi, and Beckham have all played in the World Cup tournament for their respective countries, but none have won the title. Messi came the closest

There is no doubt that Messi has experienced incredible success in tournament play; he is shown here hoisting the UEFA Champions League trophy in 2015.

with Argentina, advancing to the finals in 2014, but losing to Germany.

CLUTCH PLAYERS

Another measure of a great player is how well she or he performs when the pressure is the highest and the lights are the brightest. In the sport of soccer, no stage is bigger than the World Cup. How did each player perform during the tournament?

Player	Number of World Cup games	Goals scored	Assists
Ronaldo	17	7	2
Messi	19	6	6
Beckham	13	3	7
Pelé	14	12	2

In Ronaldo's seventeen World Cup games, he had seven goals and two assists. He was involved in nine goals, found by adding his goals and assists (7 + 2 = 9). Per game, he helped the team by scoring or assisting at a rate of .53. This is calculated by dividing his total goal involvement (goals plus assists) by the total number of games he played. For Ronaldo:

9 ÷ 17 = .53

Messi has played in nineteen World Cup games. He was involved in twelve goals (6 + 6 = 12). That gives him a scoring contribution rate of .63 per game (12 ÷ 19 = .63).

Beckham played in thirteen World Cup games for England. He scored three goals and had seven assists. This means he was involved in ten goals (3 + 7 = 10) and produced a scoring contribution rate of .76 per game (10 ÷ 13 = .76).

In fourteen World Cup games, Pelé scored twelve goals and had two assists. This means he was involved in 14 goals (12 + 2 = 14) and had an amazing scoring contribution rate of 1.0 goals per game (14 ÷ 14 = 1.0).

From this analysis, one can see that while Ronaldo has played in the most World Cup games, his scoring contribution rate is the lowest of the four players. Pelé and Beckham stepped up their games on the big stage to help their teams win, though Beckham never captured a title—while Pelé is directly responsible and was deeply involved in all three of his championship runs.

IT IS ALL ABOUT PERSPECTIVE

Which player has earned the right to be called the GOAT, the greatest of all time? Is it Ronaldo or Messi's impressive twenty-first century striking? Beckham's all-world solid play? Or Pelé's legendary scoring and indisputable championships? Each player has put together a résumé of titles and awards to support his case—so the GOAT question depends on one's point of view. While the debate continues, soccer fans can bring new elements to support their argument. Using math and statistics, they can make a rock-solid case as to why any of their favorites deserves the title of the greatest.

GLOSSARY

assist To help a player score a goal by passing him or her the ball.

Ballon d'Or An annual soccer award given to the best male player of the year.

deficiency A lack or shortage of something.

dominant Extremely powerful or influential.

ejected Kicked out; forced to leave a game.

endorsements Payments to an athlete or celebrity to promote a product or company.

icon A person or thing that has become a symbol of something.

impactful Having a major impact or effect.

legacy Something handed down by a person to the next generation.

longevity How long something lasts.

midfielder A soccer player who is responsible for getting the ball from the defense, bringing it up the field, and passing to the team's forwards.

premier First in importance or position.

prestigious Having high status and respect.

retaliated Attacked someone in response to a similar attack on oneself.

rival Another team or player competing for the same prize.

shorthanded Playing with fewer players than the opposing team.

statistic A fact or piece of data.

striker A forward in soccer who is responsible for striking the ball and shooting it at the goal.

strike rate The average number of goals scored per game.

FOR MORE INFORMATION

Canada Soccer
237 Metcalfe Street
Ottawa, ON K2P 1R2
Canada
(613) 237-7678
Website: www.canadasoccer.com
Facebook and Twitter: @CanadaSoccer
Canada Soccer is the governing body of soccer in Canada. It is a national organization that oversees the Canadian men's and women's national teams for international play.

Canadian Premier League (CPL)
Website: https://canpl.ca
Facebook, Instagram, and Twitter: @CPLsoccer
The Canadian Premier League is a professional league beginning play in April 2019 in Canada. Seven teams will compete in the inaugural season. Its website features information about the new league and its teams.

Fédération Internationale de Football Association (FIFA)
FIFA-Strasse 20
PO Box 8044 Zurich
Switzerland
+41-(0)43 222 7777
Website: http://www.fifa.com
Facebook: @FIFA
Instagram: @fifaworldcup
Twitter: @FIFAcom

FIFA is the official worldwide governing body of soccer. Its website features the latest news, national associations, competitions, results, and more in the world of soccer.

Major League Soccer (MLS)
420 Fifth Avenue, 7th Floor
New York, NY 10018
(212) 450-1200
Website: http://www.mlssoccer.com
Facebook, Instagram, and Twitter: @MLS
Major League Soccer is the professional soccer association in the United States. Its website features the latest news, information, scores, and links to teams in the league.

Premier League
30 Gloucester Place
London W1U 8PL
United Kingdom
+44 (0) 20 7864 9000
Website: http://www.premierleague.com
Facebook, Instagram, and Twitter: @PremiereLeague
The Premier League is the top level of the English football league system. Manchester United is one of the teams in the Premier League. Its website features the latest news, scores, and statistics for teams and players.

Union of European Football Associations (UEFA)
Route de Genève 46
Case Postale
CH-1260 Nyon 2
Switzerland
+41 (0) 848 04 2727
Website: http://www.uefa.com
Facebook and Twitter: @UEFA
Instagram: @uefa_official
UEFA is the governing body of European football and the umbrella organization for fifty-five national associations. Its website features the latest news, scores, and statistics for various tournaments, including the UEFA Champions League matches and more.

FOR FURTHER READING

Billioud, Jean-Michel. *Fantastic Footballers: 40 Inspiring Icons*. London, UK: Wide Eyed Editions, 2018.

Buckley, James, Jr. *Who Is Pelé?* New York, NY: Penguin Workshop, 2018.

Burshtein, Karen. *Lionel Messi: Soccer's Top Scorer*. New York, NY: Rosen Educational Services, 2018.

Hornby, Hugh and Andy Crawford. *Soccer*. New York, NY: DK Publishing, 2018.

Kelley, KC. *Top 10 Soccer Superstars*. Mankato, MN: Child's World, 2019.

Kortemeier, Todd. *Superstars of World Soccer*. Mankato, MN: Amicus High Interest, 2017.

Mikoley, Kate. *Soccer: Stats, Facts, and Figures*. New York, NY: Gareth Stevens Publishing, 2018.

Oldfield, Matt and Tom Oldfield. *Beckham: From the Playground to the Pitch*. London, UK: Dino Books, 2018.

Pettman, Kevin and Peter Liddiard. *Football Number Crunch: Figures, Facts and Soccer Stats: The World of Football in Numbers*. London, UK: Carlton Kids, 2017.

Porterfield, Jason. *Cristiano Ronaldo: Soccer Champion*. New York, NY: Rosen Educational Services, 2018.

BIBLIOGRAPHY

Beckham, David. *David Beckham—My World*. London, UK: Hodder & Stoughton, 2001.

Brewin, John. "Why Soccer Is the Most Popular Sport in the World." StadiumTalk.com, November 12, 2018. https://www.stadiumtalk.com/s/why-soccer-most-popular-sport-int-world-8145f753db7242f6.

FCTables.com. "Cristiano Ronaldo." Retrieved February 15, 2019. https://www.fctables.com/players/cristiano_ronaldo-222119.

FCTables.com. "Lionel Messi." Retrieved February 15, 2019. https://www.fctables.com/players/lionel_messi-271592.

FIFA.com. "Behind the World Cup Record: Pelé." November 21, 2016. https://www.fifa.com/worldcup/news/behind-the-world-cup-record-Pele-2852661.

FIFA.com. "Pelé: The King of Football." Retrieved February 15, 2019. https://web.archive.org/web/20160126181140/http://www.fifa.com/fifa-tournaments/players-coaches/people=63869/profile.html.

Fitzpatrick, Richard. "The Machine of '87: Messi's Boyhood Teammates Recall Early Signs of Greatness." Bleacher Report, June 23, 2017. https://bleacherreport.com/articles/2717227-the-machine-of-87-messis-boyhood-teammates-recall-early-signs-of-greatness.

Football History. "Pelé." Retrieved February 15, 2019. http://www.football-history.net/who-is-who/p/Pele.htm.

Forbes. "The World's Highest-Paid Athletes." Retrieved February 20, 2019. https://www.forbes.com/athletes/list/#tab:overall.

Goal. "Ronaldo Named Best Portuguese Player of All Time." January 15, 2015. http://www.goal.com/en/news/91/portugal/2015/01/15/7992212/ronaldo-named-best-portuguese-player-of-all-time.

Guardian staff. "David Beckham: His Club and International Career in Stats." *Guardian*, May 16, 2013. http://www.theguardian.com/football/2013/may/16/david-beckham-retires-stats-numbers.

Hayward, Ben. "The 'Little Bee' Who Always Cried—the Story of Young Ronaldo's Path to Greatness in Madeira." Goal, June 23, 2017. http://www.goal.com/en-us/news/the-little-bee-who-always-cried-the-story-of-young-ronaldos-path-/k927thno26e41b42er1z9zhqo.

Kalinic, Dejan. "Messi Is the Greatest Ever—Eto'o." Goal, September 24, 2018. http://www.goal.com/en-us/news/messi-is-the-greatest-ever-etoo/2ecugnten3zn1t4rfk06uis5x.

Kenmare, Jack. "Lionel Messi Voted the Greatest Player of All Time." SportBible, July 20, 2018. http://www.sportbible.com/football/news-reactions-legends-lionel-messi-voted-the-greatest-player-of-all-time-20180720.

Laioli, Luca. *Messi, Neymar, Ronaldo: Head to Head with the World's Greatest Players.* London, UK: Icon Books, 2014.

Transfermarkt. "Cristiano Ronaldo." Retrieved February 15, 2019. https://www.transfermarkt.com/cristiano-ronaldo/erfolge/spieler/8198.

Transfermarkt. "David Beckham." Retrieved February 15, 2019. https://www.transfermarkt.co.uk/david-beckham/nationalmannschaft/spieler/3139.

Transfermarkt. "Lionel Messi." Retrieved February 15, 2019. https://www.transfermarkt.com/lionel-messi/erfolge/spieler/28003.

Transfermarkt. "Pelé." Retrieved February 15, 2019. https://www.transfermarkt.co.uk/Pelé/erfolge/spieler/17121.

WorldAtlas. "The Most Popular Sport in the World." Retrieved March 11, 2019. https://www.worldatlas.com/articles/what-are-the-most-popular-sports-in-the-world.html.

INDEX

ABOUT THE AUTHOR

Carla Mooney is a graduate of the University of Pennsylvania. She writes for young people and is the author of many books for young adults and children. Mooney enjoys watching many sports, including World Cup soccer matches, and debating over which player is the best.

PHOTO CREDITS

Cover (top left) Daniele Badolato-Juventus FC/Getty Images; cover (top right), p. 24 Quality Sport Images/Getty Images; cover (bottom left) Ben Radford/Getty Images; cover (bottom right), p. 41 Focus On Sport/Getty Images; p. 7 charnsitr/Shutterstock.com; p. 8 John Peters/Manchester United/Getty Images; p. 10 katatonia82/Shutterstock.com; p. 14 Matthias Hangst/Getty Images; p. 17 Enrique Marcarian/REUTERS/Newscom; p. 19 Lluis Gene/AFP/Getty Images; pp. 22, 28 Bob Thomas/Getty Images; p. 26 Vlad1988/Shutterstock.com; p. 30 Victor Decolongon/Getty Images; p. 32 Eric Espada/Getty Images; p. 35 Pictorial Parade/Archive Photos/Getty Images; p. 36 © AP Images; p. 38 Popperfoto/Getty Images; p. 39 Alexander Hassenstein-FIFA/Getty Images; p. 44 Toshifumi Kitamura/AFP/Getty Images; p. 46 Nelson Almeida/AFP/Getty Images; p. 49 Ullstein Bild/Getty Images.

Design & Layout: Brian Garvey; Editor: Siyavush Saidian; Photo Researcher: Sherri Jackson